Influence through Emotional Awareness

Discover How to Develop a strong emotional awareness to improve your personality and attract people in your life

By Edward Brandon

express consent of the Publisher is provided beforehand. Any additional rights reserved.

Furthermore, the information that can be found within the pages described forthwith shall be considered both accurate and truthful when it comes to the recounting of facts. As such, any use, correct or incorrect, of the provided information will render the Publisher free of responsibility as to the actions taken outside of their direct purview. Regardless, there are zero scenarios where the original author or the Publisher can be deemed liable in any fashion for any damages or hardships that may result from any of the information discussed herein.

Additionally, the information in the following pages is intended only for informational purposes and should thus be thought of as universal. As befitting its nature, it is presented without assurance regarding its prolonged validity or interim quality. Trademarks that are mentioned are done without written consent and can in no way be considered an endorsement from the trademark holder.

Table of Contents

Introduction

Understanding human behavior isn't an easy task – you need to have the skills required to do so. Once you understand behavior, you can, influence people. Influencing people is all about persuasion. How good are you at making people follow what you say or imitate you?

This book looks at the various aspects of human behavior and how you can go ahead to make people listen to you and follow your lead. Remember that human behavior is a core component of various areas of life, including relationships, work, and many others.

To be a good persuader, you need to be patient, emotionally intelligent, be empathetic, and know when to stop. These and many more aspects of persuasion and influence are covered in this book.

Where do you think the concept of "mind-reading" came to the front? Because many people are unaware that you can influence their thoughts, but this is only possible if you have the skills to do so.

But this book is way beyond the use of persuasion and influence; it also teaches you how to apply various methods to control behavior in a specific setup. It looks at the multiple forces that guide human behavior, and when you realize that the principles are way incorporated in us that they guide our conduct each day, you will be amazed. The best thing is to know how to alter the forces so that you can use them to guide the behavior of other people.

The main issue here is how to influence people the right way so that you achieve your goals and get the right results.

The corporate world doesn't have any issue with getting information that they require to make decisions. Any manager is a click away from getting the information they need about any topic you can think of. Corporate have more information than they need and in fact, most of them have so much that they don't know which one to use and which one not to use. The only problem that we have is how to implement a strategy.

Look at meetings – many managers spend hours in meetings saying things that aren't tangible, and then everyone goes away thinking they have achieved something.

Nearly 76 percent of all the efforts in an organization fail while 65 percent doesn't remedy any action. The truth is that many people come up with plans, they document the plans, and then they fail to actualize those plans. They still use the same behavior patterns day in day out.

The right way to do things is to take concepts, then break them down into smaller principles that are more practical, and then implement them. You don't have to attend meeting after meeting, day after day to get this. Anyone can make a complicated concept, but it takes a real person to take something complicated and then make it simple and actionable.

What someone needs in such a case is to change the daily behavior. A change in a behavior arises from an influence that is exerted by someone else. For most of us, we need a push in the right direction to be able to change the way we think and do things.

For you to change your behavior, you need to be persuaded. The person to influence you must have the right emotional intelligence to identify that some change is necessary.

This book looks at everything right from behavior change to persuasion. So if you are a person stuck in a rut or you wish to be the one to influence the other person, then this is the right book for you.

Narcissistic personality

Narcissistic personality disorder has been a hot topic for the past few years. Most people have a basic understanding of it as an obsession with oneself. The tale of Narcissus tells the story of a man who fell in love with his own reflection. That is the origin of the disorder's name.

A narcissist surrounds themselves with people who will make them a priority. This means they often feed off of the emotional energy of empathetic people. They also target people with low self-esteem because they will not require much of people and accept poor treatment.

Narcissists cannot reciprocate. They take but do not give. If they need emotional support you will be expected to provide it for them for as long as they need you to, but if you are going through a rough time and need a shoulder to lean on, they will be nowhere to be found. They will not respond to your calls or messages. They will only come back around when it is yet again their turn to need something, but your turn will never come.

In a genuine relationship, the other person sees you as an equal partner and as a human being with their own feelings, and they know they will need to compromise at times. If you are in a relationship with a narcissist, they see you as a source of their narcissistic supply.

This is a term used to describe the endless amount of attention and admiration they need from others. It is a form of sustenance for them. They value you based solely on what use you can be for them, and that is exactly how they place worth on everyone in their life.

Their ego is overblown, but it is easy to bruise. It does not have to be an outright insult. For example, merely focusing on something else other than them for a moment translates in their mind to you implying they are not relevant to you.

This is because they require your undivided attention and constant validation. They cannot self-soothe, which is why you will often hear them say they are bored. If you are not giving them attention, they will gain it by pushing your buttons in an attempt to start an argument.

In this book, we will be primarily focusing on covert narcissists. A covert narcissist operates differently from an overtone. They play the victim and their narcissistic supply comes in the form of sympathy and seeing that people are willing to drop everything to help them. However, their supposed victimhood has a sinister side. If you slight them, whether it is real or perceived, which you inevitably, they will be outraged and want to "expose" you to everyone you know. The most likely source of their anger is that you tried to set a boundary with them and tell them no, which is the word a narcissist can't stand to hear.

A covert narcissist is highly manipulative. They are masters at spinning the facts into their own version of what happened to where they come out of it completely innocent you are the villain. They will tell other people you abuse them and yet they love you, so leaving you isn't an option.

This serves to bolster their martyrdom while simultaneously making you look bad in their eyes. At the same time, they will use your feelings and investment in them to get you to do what they want. This will not end until you decide to break away from them, which is often referred to in narcissistic abuse support groups as going no contact.

Getting disentangled from a narcissist is not easy. They will not like the idea of losing you because this is a narcissistic injury for them. This means you not doing what they want or being a source of what they need, will damage their inflated yet fragile opinion of themselves and their importance.

You will need to know how to deal with a smear campaign, which is often what happens to a person when they break contact with a narcissist. This means they will try to create a negative public image of you by spreading rumors and generally speaking ill of you to everyone who will listen. You must have the discipline not to retaliate because this will add fuel to the fire. If you handle this correctly, the truth will come out and it is they who will be exposed for their true selves.

If you cannot completely break contact with them, such as if there are children involved or you work with them, we will discuss different methods of dealing with someone with a narcissistic personality.

They will throw incendiary words and accusations your way, and you will have to desensitize yourself to it and just stick with the facts. For example, if they start telling you all the things you did wrong in the relationship and how difficult you were to live with, do not respond to this and simply ask if they picked up the kids.

You will also need to recover from their manipulation and abuse, especially if it took place over a long period of time. In fact, you will most likely need to go through some form of therapy because of the constant onslaught of gaslighting, berating, and many other tactics in a narcissist's bag of tricks.

One of the most effective methods of treating narcissistic abuse is Cognitive Behavioral Therapy. This will aid you in seeing the person for who they really are and recognizing what they have done to you as intolerable behavior.

It is no easy task to recover from an abusive cycle and get your life back on track, and it is something you will need to be able to commit.

However, if you stick to your principles, combat the backlash with a level head, and reach to other friends both old and new, a life free of manipulation and enriched by friends and opportunities is right around the corner.

Chapter 1: Social and Emotional-Awareness

What is social awareness?

Social awareness, as the name suggests, is that capacity to understand and respond to equally broad issues of the society as well as interpersonal struggles. This indicates that when you are socially informed, then you are very much familiar with your environment. Whatever is around or near you, and on the greater side having that ability to interpret the emotional being of the people who surround you and you constantly come in to contact with.

This concept of social awareness needs some emphasis on areas such as competency as well as empathy. In other words, we could say that social awareness is the act of internetworking of various concepts at the same time. We have theories like social sensitivity as well as social insight.

When we talk about social insight, we simply refer to the moral interpretation and the capability to understand situations with ease, whereas social sensitivity is the ability to feel for others as well as that intellect to infer. With social communication, we simply mean to mingle well with others with the aim of solving their problems and queries as they arise. In many cases, most people do equate these theories, especially the theory of social awareness and that of emotional intelligence.

Here is an example of a group of individuals having a serious discussion over a given agenda. One man comes and draws all the attention to himself minus the prior inquiry of the agenda of the meeting. In this case, he begins to learn that the meeting was aimed at solving a very critical scenario. Now only if he had known the agenda behind the meeting, that he couldn't have drawn the attention of the meeting to himself, he lacked what we call emotional intelligence.

Similarly, many other people or writers have equated the theory of emotional intelligence to that of social awareness. However, emotional intelligence relates much to that capacity to motivate others so as to mold cooperative behaviors.

We have an example of social awareness that we can explain briefly to beef up the topic.
As a person, whether a common man or a professional, you need to have powerful social awareness skills. They are vital.

Consider the following example.

Marvin is the manager of a company. She comes with a very strong agenda on the day of the staff meeting. She was to kick start the meeting very quickly. However, she realizes that there was dissatisfaction within the staff members.

She learned that from merely the staff expressions physically and emotionally. Now Marvin did not move on with the agenda of the meeting, but instead, she pauses and ask the group what the problem could be. It all came to her awareness of the various difficulties being experienced within the company.

She decides to react to it instantly, and by the conclusion of the meeting, everyone was very encouraged, and thus they showing glowing faces. She displayed the concept of social awareness.

What's Emotional Awareness?

Could you say that you are informed of your emotion? It looks like it's a joke. However, emotions are always never easily describable, as you may wish to imagine. Have you ever imagined whenever someone asks of you how you are feeling and you respond by saying that you are fine? What does it imply? Do you even mean what you say?

Definition

Emotional awareness is that capability that one has of realizing your own feelings as well as those of others. Emotional awareness is a composite of the greater picture called emotional intelligence.

Emotional intelligence includes having the ability to find solutions to pending problems in life by basically understanding people's emotions.

For example, having the ability to regulate your own personal feelings and also other people's emotions whenever they are feeling downcast.

We have people with high levels of emotional awareness. This makes someone become able to learn from his feelings.

When you are displeased with something or someone, you could instead sit back and think about it, try to trace out the cause of the annoyance and make a decision which may help solve the problem. On the other hand, you could possibly foresee the emotions in advance by noticing the leads to the very emotions, then take necessary steps to avoid them by perhaps making the right conclusions or even coming up with possible solutions.

Is Emotional Awareness Important?

Yes. It is essential to have the ability to understand your own emotional life as well as that of others. It has several advantages, of which we will revisit just but a few:

- It is easier to relay your emotions to others
- Emotions act as navigating tools which lead someone to move through his worries so easily
- It is quite easy to set your own limits that govern your working environment
- You could become your own personal doctor. You can invent an emotion meter for your own life

Whenever you have emotional awareness, it is easy for you to live a more happy life than those who lack such understanding. This is as a result of gauging between what is right and especially for you and what is not good for you. It is very evident that those people, who panic most whenever they meet challenges in life, do not have that sense of emotional awareness. They, in the long run, develop pressure, which can cause death at the end.

Relationship between Emotional Awareness and Mental Health

Whenever you lack emotional awareness, it is impossible to know how you feel. We cannot be able to understand others, and therefore, it is so impossible to control ourselves. For example, you may be feeling numb from within, or perhaps you have become so emotional, and hence you try to evade your own feelings, in this case, it clearly indicates that you have become more vulnerable to many issues of mental complications which need even more close attention. These disorders may include but not limited to: depression, anxiety, drug abuse or addictions, overeating or lack of appetite and isolation.

There are several types of emotional awareness

1. Physical sensation –behaving psychologically towards issues.
2. Action tendencies- love to make one decision.
3. Single emotions- you are either happy or sad.
4. Blend of emotions-being able to select one thing from many
5. Blend of blends of emotions- being versatile in decision-making

Social Awareness Tactics

There are various types and ways on how one would aim at improving one's self social awareness. According to the definition, social awareness we said is that the ability to precisely pick some emotions in others with an understanding of what is going on in their lives as well as yours. This is done continuously by way of listening and observation, which are the most coherent means of getting informed. When you want to listen carefully and further observe with your eyes what is going on, means that you have to forego a series of activities which you are supposed to be doing, talking about, stop thinking loudly, stop guessing whatever has not been said by theater party and perhaps stop thinking quickly.

There are several tactics that help improve our knowledge of social awareness capacity.

i. Avoiding taking notes at meeting places

If you take notes whenever in a meeting place, your attention to the mood of the room and that concentration to others gets destructed. By not taking notes, therefore, it increases that capacity to concentrate on other things. However, much note-taking is helpful; it destructs our attention to others. Therefore we won't have that social awareness. Notes are critical; however,

24

if you have to take notes especially during a practical lesson, then you need to pause at a given interval and give yourself room for observation which is also as good as taking notes. Just jade down some keywords or put your entire writing in summary format in order to give yourself time or room to listen and observe what the leader or others are doing. You will be able to utilize your social awareness skills.

ii. Be Empathetic

Empathy is that aspect of feeling for others. Just put yourself in someone's shoe. It is straightforward to have someone feel that you are with them emotionally by the way you express yourself to them, the attention you give to people in their respective situations.

iii. Ask Closely Related Questions

This is ever called a back pocket question. Sometimes when someone is going through a tough time say n sickness or some emotional torture, it is very evident that they may not be so willing to open up to you for fear of some reasons best known to them. In the context of back pocket questioning, you ask something that is just closely related to the circumstance or tries to come up with a similar scenario. The person in question will begin opening up as he contributes to the topic. At the end of it all, he will be open to you and even reveal to you the matter that is causing discomfort.

Chapter 2: How to Win Friends

Having friends is considered an integral aspect of one's social lives. A good network of friends can enable one to cope with some of the days to day challenges of life while at the same time, encourage one to develop positive behavior such as making regular visits to the gym. Friends also play a key role in assisting one to recover from adverse situations such as financial or health-related complications. This chapter will explain several approaches that you can use in order to win and retain friends. In particular, the section will look at the impact of influence and persuasion in enhancing your ability to win friends. Secondly, the discussion will also focus on the various approaches that can be applied in order to attract the interest of potential friends.

One of the essential aspects when it comes to attracting and retaining friends relates to the manner in which a person thinks.

It is often said that people with the same thought process are more likely to establish a sustainable friendship relationship. In light of this fact, it is imperative to align your way of thinking with the people that you want to befriend. Ideally, such an approach should enable one to identify some of the issues that are important with respect to the lives of the people they would wish to be friends with. Furthermore, you will be in a better position to develop similar interests, and this will significantly enhance your capacity to develop a sustainable friendship with the people you like.

One of the things that break or undermines most friendships is dishonesty and manipulation. Many people might prefer to lie about their backgrounds, their profession, value systems, and other integral aspects of their lives in order to attract friends.

Similarly, some people can also resort to flattery and false praises as a means of attracting and retaining friends. Such an approach is defined as manipulation, and it is not very useful since one will eventually end up losing friends when they find out the truth.

In light of this fact, this chapter will also focus on how to use positive influence and not manipulation to win friends.

How Influence and Persuasion Can Help To Win Friends

Be Friendly

Influence and persuasion can go a long way in enabling someone to win and attract friends. First and foremost, in order to influence and persuade other people to fall within your circle of friends, you must be friendly to them.

A friendly disposition is a fundamental requirement that makes someone quite attractive to other people, thus resulting in long-lasting relationships. There are various ways through which one can manifest a friendly disposition. Your body language is perhaps one of the most central aspects that can enable you to cultivate a friendly disposition.

For instance, learning to smile once every so often whenever interacting with other people is considered a vital aspect of an effective body language. A smile can go a long way in making other people feel secure whenever they are around you, which will, in turn, enable you to earn their trust.

Furthermore, leaning forward and maintaining eye contact during conversations is also an appropriate body language that tells other people that you are indeed an approachable person who can quickly get along with other people. All in all, being

31

friendly to other people through the use of appropriate body language will ensure that you are able to influence their perception of what they think about you thus enhancing your ability to make friends.

Advise but Do Not Criticize

Many people do not take kindly to criticism. Most often than not, people would want to be made to feel that their position on any issue is the correct one, but this is not always the case. Persuasion and influence are essential when you want to correct other people or offer an alternative perspective from the one that they might be having.

However, the approach you use will determine whether or not you can win over other people and ensure that they are on your side. Avoid criticizing at any cost and instead, offer your advice as an alternative way of looking at the issue. In the same breath, it is equally important to point out that you agree with the perspective of others before outlining areas that you think might need some further improvements.

For instance, while engaging in a political argument with someone else, you can agree with their perspective but go a step further by outlining some of the additional policies that you think can be implemented in order to improve the current political environment. This approach will enable you to put across your views on the matter without necessarily having to criticize the opinions expressed by those around you.

Be a Good Role Model

The saying birds of a feather flock together applies very well when it comes to friendships. This simply means that people usually tend to identify with other people with whom they share common values and principles.

Being a good role model can enable one to cultivate the right values that will allow them to attract many friends. For instance, values such as honesty, hard work, and commitment are considered universally attractive and can go a long way in making one a good role model in society.

Espousing such values, therefore, makes one attractive to other people who also cherish such them thus making one to act as a role model. For instance, it is quite common to find that the circle of friends of a successful CEO comprises of equally high accomplishing individuals.

This is because all of them value hard work and commitment with these values being the glue that holds them together. Being a good role model accords one an opportunity to define who they are and attract like-minded individuals within their circle of friends.

Make Other People Feel Important

In order to influence, persuade, and win over other people, you must make them feel that they matter. Another person can only identify themselves as your friend if they are made to feel that they matter to you.

This is very important, especially when it comes to relationships between individuals who might not be at the same status in life. For instance, the CEO of a high profile company can only establish a friendship relationship with low cadre employees such as the janitors if the former actually go out of their way to instill some level of self-confidence and high self-esteem on the part of the janitors. In this example, the CEO can schedule periodic meetings with all categories of employees, including the very junior ones so that they can be able to interact and exchange ideas on issues affecting the company freely.

By doing this, the CEO will make the janitors and all other low-level employees feel equally important within the organizational setting. The CEO will thus be in a better position to establish a long-lasting friendship with their employees, consequently, creating the kind of synergy that will enhance overall organizational performance.

How to Interest People

Being able to draw the attention and interest of other people is a valuable tip when it comes to your ability to win friends. People must be able to identify with you before they can commit to being your friend. It is therefore vital that you are in a position to take various steps that will make them realize who you are, what you stand for, and make them understand that your ideas actually resonates with theirs.

In order to sell your ideas to others, you have to capture their interest and be able to make them understand that whatever it is that you are proposing is something that will actually add value to their lives.

Identify With Their Issues

Most people will be interested in what you have to say or your opinion on something if you are talking about an issue that they identify with. Different people are faced with various problems, and it is vital to understand some of their issues in order to interest other people.

This is despite the fact that some that you might not be experiencing some of the problems in question. For instance, you might be coming from a wealthy background and thus not facing any socio-economic issues.

However, someone that you wish to befriend might be coming from a poor background and is faced with a myriad of socio-economic challenges. In such a scenario, the most effective way to earn their interest is to identify with some of the challenges that they are facing even if your circumstances are different.

This might entail letting them know that you know what they are going through and that you are willing to offer them any assistance that they might need.

Sometimes, the assistance might not even be in the form of material support. This is because some of the issues that other people are experiencing might not necessarily relate to material things but more to do with their emotional state. For instance, someone might be experiencing an emotional breakdown or even depression.

Like a good friend or a potential one, all you need to do is to offer them advice and the necessary assurance that all will be fine.

Be a Good Listener

Listening is one of the more vital soft skills that can help enhance interpersonal relationships, but it is often ignored. The best way to learn more about other people is by listening to them.

By listening to other people, you will be able to identify the challenges that they might be facing, their goals and objectives in life, their fears, hobbies and additional vital information that will improve your capacity to interact with them and form mutually beneficial relationships.

A true friend is one who actually takes the time to know the other person and strive to be a better friend each and every other day. For example, if you know some of the goals and objectives of another person, then you will be in a better position to assist them in the attainment of the same. In turn, the other person will appreciate you much more and consider you to be their true friend.

Furthermore, by having an understanding of another person's fears and challenges, you will be able to avert situations that might result activate such fears.

Know People by Their Names

People usually find it interesting when you refer to them by their names, especially during your initial interaction. Many people might assume that you do not know them by their names, but once you refer to them by their names, they get surprised and will be more than willing to indulge you.

Furthermore, it is very annoying when someone within your social setting knows you by your name, but somehow, you cannot seem to remember theirs.

For instance, a colleague at work might refer to you by your name and put you in an awkward position as far as the interaction is concerned since you cannot seem to remember their names.

In such a situation, the other person might dismiss you as an arrogant or a self-centered individual who does not pay significant attention to other people.

You might probably never be able to win their interest if this is the case. Therefore, knowing other people's names and refereeing to them by their names during initial interactions can be the premise of a long-lasting friendship.

This is because, they will feel appreciated since someone else actually took the time to know their names and in turn, they will appreciate you for that.

They will be more likely to listen keenly to what you have to say, respond positively to any reasonable request and even be willing to accept future engagements such as a date, meeting or night out request.

Share a Personal Story

Friendship is mainly all about trust. This implies that two people who call each other friends should be able to trust one another, sometimes with their deepest secrets.

However, it takes a considerable amount of time before such trust can be earned. It has been established that one of the fastest ways to earn the trust of another person is to open up yourself to them by sharing something personal relating to your life. Many people might fear to do so since it might make them vulnerable to other people.

However, if done the right way, it should enable you to win the interest and trust of the other person. A correct approach would, for instance, allowing other people a peep into your personal life by telling them something that is close to you but one that can nonetheless be used by a malicious person to undermine your reputation.

This might be something as mundane as your personal phobias that you might not have previously shared with anyone else. By sharing such information, the other person will definitely take much more interest in you, but at the same time, trust you with their personal stories.

How to Win People with Your Way of Thinking

The power to convince other people to see your point of view is vital when it comes to winning friends. A friend should not only be someone who you interact with and share fun experiences with, but they should also be your allies in life.

A partner in this context basically means someone who is ready to stand by you, defend you and your ideas, and collaborate with you towards the realization of a mutually beneficial objective.

Being able to have your friends as your allies is useful even in an economic context. For instance, you might be having a sound business plan on how you on a start-up with great potential. However, you realize that you cannot attain this objective on your own.

In such a scenario, you are most likely to reach out to those people you consider friends and share with them your thoughts about the start-up and convince them to embrace your idea as their very own.

Elaborately Express Your Thoughts and Ideas

Before you can even dream of convincing other people to adopt your thought process and ideas, you must first and foremost explain to them what they are. Such explanation must not be plain and boring; instead, it has to be elaborate.

This implies that you have to employ various techniques that will capture the attention of the people you are interacting with while at the same time, enhancing their overall understanding of the issue that you are trying to put across.

For instance, you might have to employ the use of gestures and appropriate facial expressions that illustrate various human emotions such as excitement, anger, and happiness. You can also use graphic images such as photos and videos that relate to the issue that you are concerned about.

The use of statistical data can also significantly elaborate your thoughts and ideas. For example, if you are trying to come up with a business idea that will address the issue of obesity in the country, you might want to present to them figures from the appropriate National agency that highlights the prevalence of obesity in the country.

Being elaborate in the manner in which you interact with other people and present issues will enhance their understanding of perspective.

Your friends will be much more willing to identify with your ideas, own them and even go a step further in providing you the financial and other assistance that you might need in order to implement various solutions.

Make Room for Divergent Opinions

Whenever you are interacting with other people, you have to take time and listen to their points of view as well. Some of your friends and other people you are communicating with might be hesitant to embrace your way of thinking.

Such people will have their own divergent opinions on the issue, and you must know how to go about addressing such views. In such a scenario, it is crucial to listen to what they have to say and use this information to build a consensus.

Some people make the mistake of insisting on having their way and not making any compromises. The 'my way or the highway' approach is a recipe for disaster since many people will end up seeing you as dictatorial and consequently, they will not want to have anything to do with you or your ideas.

However, when you are able to listen to divergent views, you will be in a position to relate such opinions with your own thoughts and establish common grounds between you and your friends. By doing so, the other people will be able to identify with your thoughts on the issue since you will have addressed any issues, concerns, and reservations that they might have on the same.

Integrating the ideas of others within your own will definitely make it easy for them to embrace your way of thinking; furthermore, it can also help you improve your thought process. This is because; other people are likely to bring to the table an issue or a perspective that might have escaped your mind while formulating your idea. The overall output would, therefore, be a much more refined idea and an improved thought process on your part.

Never Dismiss Others

While it is true that some of your colleagues, friends, and people you interact with might have different ideas and thoughts on an issue that can improve your own, this is not always the case.

There are those who are likely to put forward suggestions that might totally deviate from the position that you hold. For instance, using the aforementioned example of obesity, one of your friends might be of the view that obesity and other lifestyle diseases are a non-issue in the country.

Such a view is obviously wrong, and for this reason, you might be tempted to dismiss them blatantly. However, it is always imperative to remember to resist such a temptation at all cost. This is because rejecting the ideas of other people might encourage them to reciprocate the gesture and also deny whatever you have to say even if they know it is the correct position.

Instead of rejecting, it is better to try and convince them using other ways to embrace your thoughts on the issue. In case everything fails and the other party still holds onto their position in the issue, you can simply promise to take another look into the topic thus ensuring that the problem is solved in an amicable manner.

Illustrate Benefits Associated With Your Way Of Thinking

Many people would wish to derive some sort of benefit from whatever engagement that they undertake. Bonus, especially financial incentive, is therefore considered a strong motivator, and as such, you should strive to illustrate some of the potential benefits that others can derive by adopting your way of thinking. A good example would perhaps be the debate on sustainability.

Sustainability, especially within the corporate space, is increasingly becoming a hot topic with many people holing the view that companies should take proactive measures to ensures that their operations do not harm the environment.

However, there are equally as many people who do not buy into the idea of sustainability, especially on the need for corporate to significantly alter their operations in order to cater to environmental sustainability concerns.

In such a scenario, you can illustrate some of the benefits that the company might accrue by adopting a sustainable approach to business. For instance, you can point out the fact that sustainable sourcing for raw material will enhance its availability in the long-run outlook of the organization. Your capacity to illustrate such benefits will attract the attention of others and make them embrace your line of thought, thus improving the nature of the relationship that you share with them.

How to Use Positive Influence and Not Manipulation to Win Friends

Both positive influence and manipulation can be deployed by anyone wishing to win friends. The positive influence will enable one to establish a long-lasting friendship with other people. Manipulation, on the other hand, can allow one to win friends; however, such bonds do not often stand the test of time.

This is because manipulation usually entails some form of lies being peddled around designed to make the other person have a distorted opinion of who you are.

Similarly, manipulation can also be in the form of you pretending to be someone you are not in order to attract other people and win their friendship. Sooner or later, such people are bound to see your true colors, and once this happens, they will most likely terminate the friendship.

In light of this fact, having a positive impact on the life of another person is perhaps the most appropriate approach to establish long-lasting friendships. This section will highlight five ways through which you can use positive influence instead of manipulation to win over friends.

Be Compassionate and Caring

People experience trying times at various stages in their lives. One of the best ways to use positive influence to win over friends is to offer them a shoulder to lean on when they truly need it. Simply put, you should be compassionate with them whenever they are faced with difficult times, such as going through the loss of a loved one.

Try to relate to the pain that they are going through and offer both emotional and physical support when necessary. Being compassionate and caring during difficult times to someone else will endear them to you, and they are likely to reach out and establish a long-lasting friendship with you.

Show Appreciation

Positive influence also requires one to appreciate other people for whom and what they are. People have different positive and negative attributes. In order to win friends, you should focus more on highlighting the positive qualities of other people since this will make them attracted to you and eventually, become your friends. Furthermore, it is essential to appreciate the fact that many people usually go out of their way to improve various aspects of their lives, including their professional lives, social lives, and even overall health.

In such a situation, you should ensure that show your appreciation for the efforts ad improvements that other people are taking in order to improve their lives. This might simply be in the form of a simple congratulatory message conveyed to the person on their particular achievement in life or their endeavors. Showing appreciation to other people is one way through which positive influence can help one win friends since they will be able to know that you are genuinely concerned about their overall well being and that you are proud of their achievements.

Do Not Flatter

As much as it is essential to show appreciation with respect to the achievements and endeavors of others, you never use flattery. Flatter refers to false praise that is offered to someone with an objective of influencing their way of thinking. For instance, a junior employee might need a favor from their senior colleague. Instead of asking for the support, the employee might resort to offering false praises to their senior in order to be in good terms with before asking for the favor.

Flattery does not constitute genuine appreciation since it is not sincere. Instead, flattery is more or less a form of manipulation whereby you congratulate someone on a false pretext or over-exaggerate their achievement in order to be in their good terms with them. Flattery just like any other form of manipulation might enable one to win friends, but also this will be short-lived since people are bound to find out one way or the other about the false praises that they have been offered.

Strive To Have A Positive Impact On Others

It is crucial to ensure that your presence in the life of other people should have a profound impact on their lives. Literally speaking, positive influence will see other people experience a positive transformation in their lives on account of your presence. For instance, the positive impact might be in the form of investment advice to your colleagues occasioned by your expertise in the field. Like a good friend or potential friend, you can offer the best advice based on your area of expertise, for instance, investment advice to someone who is a novice in the area.

This is an excellent example of how you can positively impact the life of another person, and thus, such a person will most likely establish a long-lasting friendship with you. Similarly, positive influence can also be in the form of advice that is meant to improve the social and overall well being of the person in question. For example, you might notice that your colleague is getting into an anti-social habit such as alcoholism or drug use. In this case, as a good friend, you should intervene and ensure that this trend is reverted in a timely manner so as to avert a situation where your colleague ends up experiencing dire consequences in their social and overall well being.

Your intervention will constitute a positive impact on the life of your colleague, which might see the two of you becoming lifelong friends.

Conclusion

To sum it all up, the knowledge on how to win friends can be integral in helping one enhance their social lives. In addition to being lifelong companions, friends can also enable one to adopt various positive behavior changes such as proper lifestyle choices that will improve their overall well being. This chapter has discussed different approaches that can be applied in order to win and maintain friends. First and foremost, you can use influence and persuasion as an approach to win over friends. Influence and persuasion entail being friendly to other people, making other people feel important and offering advice in a considerate manner.

Secondly, winning over friends can also be achieved by attracting the interest of other people. Many people would like to identify with someone they find interesting, and there are several ways through which you can capture the attention of potential friends. Some of these approaches include: identifying with their issues, being a good listener, knowing other people's names, and even sharing some interesting personal information about you with others. It is not only enough to win over friends, but it is equally important to be able to develop the capacity to influence other people with your way of thinking.

Many people are more likely to befriend you if they relate to the manner in which you think. In order to influence other people with your way of thinking, you should elaborately express your thoughts and ideas, make room for divergent opinions, and avoid dismissing other people. Furthermore, in order to win friends, you should strive to be a positive influence and avoid using manipulation. Being a positive influence implies having a positive impact on people's lives. You can also ensure that you regularly express appreciation for their achievements in order to encourage them to continue reaching for more. Finally, avoid flattery since this is considered a form of manipulation which cannot result in a long-term friendship.

Chapter 3: How to Develop a Likeable Personality

a. Trust and Honesty

Most people have a misleading notion that for one to be likable, it is a natural thing or unteachable character which has but very few people. When you are honest, honest, and trustworthy, it calls for more people to invest in you. This means that you are open and transparent in everything that you do. Everyone needs someone with character, or rather many people desire to have these characteristics, but it is impossible for them all come with their own cost. A likable person should be trustworthy and also honest. Speaking the truth, giving correct accountability of issues, being open in decision making, and also being genuine as well as usable creates a likable character in you.

b. Empathy

The skill to comprehend and share the feelings of another. Consider a society where at all times your known for your empathetic characters. This is very good. Everyone would wish to associate with you. It is a unique character. It is a likable trait. Whenever you show that kindness to people, they definitely develop the liking towards you automatically. You can be liked for being empathetic with people.

C. Conflict Resolution

What is the conflict? This could be defined as an occurrence that creates a sense of misconceptions among people. It is a conflict of interest whenever people are fighting over property or a piece of valuable material. Judges have always taken up the role of conflict resolutions. However, there is a notion of bias that makes them not likable as a result of being bribed by a big party. A conflict resolver must not take sides. He should be just and balanced in making judgments. If you are a just resolver of conflicts, you will be likable. It takes a great deal with wisdom to be likable.

d. Open-mindedness

This is all about thinking outside the box. You need not be tied entirely on the arising event. The notion of open-mindedness is a very key component of mental intelligence. People often like those who can offer relevant solutions to the pending problems by predicting or forecasting whatever the consequences of the underlying challenge will lead to. They are the ones who will openly without fear or favor give the predictions of the end results o the underlying issues. In other words, they are solution givers and not problem escalators. They do give out their minds pertaining to problems genuinely.

e. Sense of Humor

There are some situations in life which call for someone to shift attention from the main issue to a more pleasing problem. Being humorous means being funny; you make people laugh even though the situation at hand is not a laughing matter. This is all about spicing up the topic for some sense to come in, especially when people have reached loggerheads.

Even in organizations, there are different types of leaders: those who are humorous and those who look so severe. People may tend to like so much the bosses who are more humorous as compared to the tough ones. Suppose someone has committed a felony that is worthy of punishment. A lead comes and cracks over it as he tries to resolve the matter; in this case, the employee will feel released and very remorseful. He will easily learn from his mistake, never to repeat it again, on the contrary, if the boss handles the matter, pointing out sharply, the person who did it and even embarrassing the employee, it could make the employee become nervous, hence breaking down emotionally. Whenever someone breaks down emotionally, he needs emotional treatment through counseling. This is an extra cost.

He won't be productive anymore. He needs time to heal psychologically; hence, this will be eating into the organization's time and productivity. Similarly, bosses who are humorous are more likable compared to those of which are so serious and gloomy.

f. Good Manners

Good manners is a broad term or are the summary of all that we have discussed before. Whenever you behave well before people, it shows a sign of discipline. This reveals that even when you are entrusted with someone's wealth, you can handle it with caution. You will be liked by many for the character that you display before them.

When you are disciplined, you have some characteristics which are unique to society. Everybody wishes to be disciplined; even if they are not, they still think they are. There are some characteristics of a disciplined person that are attractive to many people. For example:

- Honest

- Trustworthy

- Kind

- Open

- Soft-spoken not rough

- Friendly

- Time manager

- Assertive

- Dependable

- Slow to anger

- Forgiving

- And many more

All these among many others are qualities of a disciplined person. Such attributes, one does not acquire from school or having a very high level of education. Most of these traits are dependent on the nature of your upbringing and on the greater side are influenced by the societies that we live in. the environment, people we associate with most and perhaps the jobs that we are doing.

Another trigger of the behavioral changes could be our individual perspective of things. We can grow our characters by simply being influenced by what we are earning, opportunities for improvement or deterioration, our peers or the people we hang out with. These among many other factors can affect our general mannerism and how we behave towards other people.

No one, however, is interested in bad manners though it happens like sicknesses or disease. We have a great interest in making ourselves likable by many as a result of good manners.

Become A Storyteller to Get Attention (By Including Humor And Stimulate Imagination)

By becoming a storyteller, it does not mean that you become invalid or derail from the main agenda of the day into storytelling.

Storytelling is a method of passing a message or information to the target group or category of people in a more user-friendly and more attractive way. We believe that everyone likes stories. By the use of the storytelling method to convey messages or information, it means that you have a high imaginative capacity. Usually referred to as the "Think Big Strategy."

Storytelling is not a profession. So anyone can be a storyteller. Many people, who use storytelling as a means of communication, are ever liked by masses. Take an example of a politician who is used to deliver his points home by use of narratives; you find that, locally everybody will wish to be at that particular point in time when the message is being passed. Storytelling is attractive and educative, as well. One person gets the topic, tries to relate it with another event that occurred, seeks to add some creativity in it through stimulate imagination and evaluation, and then he organizes his literature very well on how he will deliver the message at long last. Stories act as emotional drugs. They help relieve some people from their stresses and reduce pressures.

In organizations, during the times of presentations, many people or leaders opt to use this method of storytelling as opening remarks or even in the middle of a presentation as an ice breaker. If he uses it at the end of the performance, he leaves the congregation even more captivated by the topic than when he just rests his case and sits down. If he uses it at the beginning, it acts as an eye-opener and makes the audience more interested. A story is fundamental, especially in the midst of the presentation for it help relieve the audience from too much concentration, which, may result in total deviation or brain stress. Whenever you put a lot of focus on an event or subject, the chances are that you may not capture all that is being passed across. Your brain needs some rest to create more room for concentration.

Take an example of a boss who comes into an office where everyone is busy working on his annual report. Very busy they are, and as a result, no one is talking to the other. He begins a story that captivates all workers, and hence ever one lifts his head high. In the same story, he cracks a joke that leaves all people teeth out. It is a perfect thing so that even if he passes across a deadline message, it won't be taken lightly but instead with a lot of seriousness in a friendly way.

Chapter 4 –Influence and Leading without Authority

Leadership

This is the capacity of having others follow you minus any form of power. It is the way you influence people; it does not matter if you are at a place of authority or not. To lead in other terms or words can be used to mean influence. To leading in many occasions has been used interchangeably with influencing. In this context, we could just have an overview of the situation where one obligated to lead without any form of authority or power. There are questions that one may come up with because in typical circumstances, whenever a leader is chosen or appointed or elected, there must be a set of rules and regulations which govern on his way of leadership.

In a country, we can talk of the constitution that has been laid down to help leaders in their governance. However, whenever rules are set in any given institution, they must be followed strictly and also they must be ell explained to the members of that organization whatsoever to avoid conflicts of interest.

On the other hand, there are situations where you can be assigned the role of leadership, yet no principles to govern your leadership strategy. That is what we are going to lay our focus in the next chapters.

Tactics to Influence without Authority

1. Creation of A Mutual Setting

By creating an environment that is more of collaborative than stand-alone, mean that you need to act on some aspects. You need to leave the sense of self at the doorway. In this, we mean that sometimes people or leaders would always want their subjects to know their nature of the operation and how strict or tough or time-bound they are. However, that only happens in an environment where there is room to exercise power or authority. Many are times where you could hear leaders saying statements like, "they must know who I am today!" such sentiments only applies where there are traces of authority given to its leaders.

But in this format, you need to be selfless for you to be effective.

Again passion is very crucial. You need to have passion for whatever you are doing. You need to have an interest in the people you are, leading. When you have a passion for them, I mean that you will definitely love them and like what they are doing. In the long run, they will also love you

You need to come up with a single form of authority. Not everyone under you should exercise authority. You could instead come up with a specific unique structure which will help you in your governance.

2. Preparedness

You must be able to define your audience in advance. This helps you have courage in your roles as a leader. It takes away the fear because you will have gotten used to the people you are leading.

In the same way, you need to devise answers to the underlying questions within the setup. This helps eliminate unnecessary doubts from within the multitudes hence paving the way for your effective leadership.

It is imperative to plan ahead of time. Things may become very challenging if you do not plan for them ahead of time. This helps solve the puzzle of time wastage and also alleviating the inevitable as they come up. Else if you do not organize yourself very well, you risk failing.

3. Be a Facilitator

You need to be a team leader who is as well a team player. This motivates the audience to follow the trends and gives them courage on what they are doing as well as confidence.

Whenever you facilitate the exercises, you will be motivating them and also communicating with them in a manner they feel appreciated and loved.

However, you shouldn't overplay in the events. This will lead to overinvestment in you in terms of outcomes. They will tend to rely on your ability for every result they get. They will tend to imagine that all results were influenced by you and as such, heavily rely upon your input for their performance.

How to Criticize Without Being Hated

Feedback in any organization is vital and must be there for systems to work perfectly well. Employees need to receive feedback regularly as far as their jobs are concerned. And more especially, as far as, their overall performance is concerned. It has been a trend in many organizations to relay the criticisms or feedback to employees in a more formal way every time it arises. However, sometimes, this may not work depending on the nature of the feedback.

In recent survey as indicated on the Harvard Business Review blog, in one of the postings, it was noted that some employees would opt to get their feedback, however negative they are, in a more constructive criticism way rather than very positive feedback. This is associated with their belief that it would improve on their job performance. We have found out that most people do not like receiving negative feedback; however, negative feedback is important as long as it is packaged and delivered well. It is good for improvement.

a)   Feedback should be given on the basis of real behavior, not imaginary stories. When giving feedback, constructive feedback is based on actual facts and figures, not general assumptions of how a person perceives the other. For example, if an employee is deemed to be underperforming, as a leader, you need to point out the exact causes leading to underperformance like late submission of reports, and not allegations like you are very lazy.

b)   Avoid beating about the bush. Good leaders will always precise, specific, and straight to the point. This drives the point home easily; else, the employee may become confused and fail to understand your objective. The employee may feel that you were too personal on him.

c)   Suggest relevant examples and possible alternative ways of improvement. If the employee knows where he erred, he should be given as well possible remedies to the same. It motivates him most.

d)   Tone. While passing the information concerning the negative feedback, learn to use a proper tone that does not mean to harm. Even though the boss is very annoyed with the employee's performance, he needs to use a socially receptive tone that seems friendly to the employee in question. This will help alleviate the problem than molding it.

e)   Identify the proper timing of the real event. Timing is very important. Constructive criticism can yield good fruits if delivered at the right time as far as the recipient is concerned. The managers should not as well delay so much in issuing out the constructive criticisms for they will tend to forget the basics and hence embark on other objective making the whole exercise unfriendly.

f)   Medium of communication. Managers need to embrace the so tempting face to face conversations. However, tempting it could be, it still carries the day. The employees will be so encouraged for they will also be given room for explanation. continuously, in turn, builds confidence in the employee towards his bosses as opposed to a very frustrating and embarrassing phone call or email.

Different Types of Influences

There are different types of influences that can be used to achieve the same results as above. We will look at each one of them briefly in the text format.

i. Positional Influence

Positional influence is very key in delivering constructive feedback to the organization. As the top boss or the CEO of a company, you need to act as the role model to the workers. Assume you are the one in that position of your worker. Handle the worker as your equal but not in a light manner. Be user-friendly. Let the employees know that you are aware of the performance positions of every employee and that you are concerned with their well being. Do not be so harsh or react in a manner that depicts that you are the overall decision-maker

ii. Expertise Influence

Whenever you have that level of expertise, it is good to assume that not all employees have a similar experience. Handle the cases in a more professional way. Correct practically as if you are teaching them for the first time. They will want to associate with the person who has some expertise in the right field for the term to be challenged.

iii. Resources Influence

Use the available resources to pass the communication to the employees. Resources are vital because if you use the resource influence to take constructive criticism, then it is easier for the employee to grasp the content and become more resourceful to the company.

iv. Informational Influence

If you have access to various types of information within the organization, it is perfect to merge this information as relates specific issue or person for better results. Knowledge is power. Always when trying to pass information, use the right means, and always aim at resolving conflicts.

V. Direct Influence

If you have a direct link with the employees, be sure what you relay to them. If you are involved directly in what they do, you should act as a guide to them and not as a supervisor. They will want to listen to you much when being guided as opposed to when being criticized.

vi. *Relationship Influence*

A relationship is significant to any organization. It determines how good you can work with one another. Whenever you create a good relationship with the employees, they can be so willing to associate with you, and as such, it is easier rely a message to them whether good or bad depending on the nature of communication.

Chapter 5: Covert Emotional Manipulation

We've all heard about manipulation. You've seen it talked about on psychology talk shows. You've had it happen to you before and you know it makes you feel uncomfortable. You might have friends or be in a relationship with someone who often makes you feel confused and like your mind is being jerked around.

They try to control you instead of treating you like a real person whose opinions they respect. Arguing with them feels different from arguments with other people. For them, it is about winning the fight, and they always do, and the tactics they use don't seem fair. You don't feel like you have any other choice than to give in to what they want. When this is happening to you, you are not having an argument. You are a victim of covert emotional manipulation.

Manipulation is the tactic a person uses when, for whatever reason, they cannot simply say what they want. They might have a problem asking for things outright because to them it feels like they are too bold. Maybe they have the self-awareness to realize what they are trying to get you to do is selfish and will come at a personal cost to you, and so asking you in a straightforward way would most likely be met with a no. For some people, manipulation is a hobby.

They get the same pleasure from it as others get from playing tennis, sewing, or logging into their video game accounts. In any of these cases, they try to figure out ways to get what they want without having to verbalize it. Manipulation is also a means of keeping a person under their control. In fact, it is the essential purpose of the act. They do not feel any personal power so they must take it from other people.

For some people, their narcissistic personality disorder is so severe that they use manipulation tactics to pass the time. This comes from something sometimes referred to as narcissistic boredom. They enjoy playing mind games with people and get a good feeling from the conflicts that arise from them. It is a means of causing drama, which narcissists love to do, even if they say they do not.

You probably remember that person in high school who always had some kind of argument going on with at least one person, and yet they would claim to hate drama and then say they don't know why it always follows them wherever they go. You might know someone like this even now. This is actually just to gain more attention because they are looking for sympathy for the hardships they are going through, even though they have brought these difficult times onto themselves. Having a constant series of arguments with others means the attention always has to be centered on them: they need someone to vent to because their day was so difficult, they need you to give them advice, you need to console them about something the other person said, the list goes on.

Narcissists also have a habit of keeping the atmosphere in a constant heightened state of tension. They like to have others around them feeling uncomfortable because it makes them feel powerful. If they have the ability to make everyone in the room feel on edge, they are important. That is the core issue with a narcissist, especially a covert one. They do not feel relevant to anyone. This is why they need constant validation.

Manipulative behavior can take many forms. The tactics of an overt narcissist are easy to pinpoint because they will likely be loud and aggressive. For a covert narcissist, the tactics are insidious. Often, they even come to you disguised as someone who needs your help. They know that the things they tell you will bring out your protective instincts. They play on the empathetic nature of people to get attention from them. Like a fishing hook floating in the water with bait attached, waiting for a fish to bite, the covert narcissist waits for a compassionate soul to come along. The moment you decide you are going to be their caretaker is the moment they begin their designs on you.

Attention-seeking behaviors are common among those with a narcissistic personality disorder, especially of the covert form. Because of this, it can often be confused with histrionic personality disorder, and they share certain identifying behaviors- the aforementioned attention-seeking behaviors, and egocentrism. For covert narcissists, they often emulate the symptoms of mental disorders such as depression and anxiety so that the attention always has to be on them. It is despicable of a person to use disorders they know nothing about to gain attention and sympathy for others. These behaviors are what make it difficult for those who are genuinely struggling with depression to come forward. They are afraid to seek help out of the fear that they will be accused of "doing it for attention". Just as people who fabricate stories of being attacked by outside forces undermine the credibility of real victims, people who tell false stories of internal demons prevent people who are truly suffering from getting the help they need.

A covert narcissist needs a constant flow of emotional support. You cannot give your emotional support to another person indefinitely. You might tell them you cannot talk today because you either have something you need to do or you simply do not have the emotional energy it would take to be their caregiver today. One of a few things will happen to you. They might try to make you feel guilty for leaving them when they need you. They might also use emotionally charged words to manipulate you into giving them what they want. Emotionally charged words are intended to make you feel forced to do something. In the case of a covert narcissist, they will probably say something like "I wouldn't call unless it was an emergency."

Covert emotional manipulation also often takes the form of using shame tactics. If you try to do something for yourself, they will act like you are doing something selfish that comes at their expense. This will especially happen if you decide to set a boundary with them. You might feel guilty about feeling like they are a leech, but your instincts are right. There is such a thing as a person asking too much of you. If you are a highly empathetic person it may be hard to realize when someone is taking advantage of you.

Sometimes in a particularly insidious form of manipulation, the person will lead you into a trap. For example, they might ask you if you want a donut. You say yes, and then after you have accepted and eaten it, they begin complaining about how they wish they had a donut of their own, but they gave their last one away. While they will not say it, they strongly imply it- you took their last donut. You are then supposed to feel guilty about this because it is your fault. They think you should have known you were taking too much from them. It is their way of subtly attacking you and at the same time prompting you to have sympathy for them. It is time for you to pay for your crimes against them.

One of the most common forms of covert emotional manipulation in a relationship can be summarized with this phrase. "If you love me, you will (insert what they want you to do or give them here)." This phrase is highly manipulative because it puts you in an impossible situation. You don't want to do whatever they are asking of you, but they are saying if you don't do it, they will feel like you do not love them.

This is a painful thought because you do love this person and they are taking advantage of that fact to try to lead you to do what they want. In emotional manipulation, the feelings the person is putting on display feelings they are not actually experiencing.

That is the basis of what emotional manipulation is. It is when a person wants something from someone else that has been denied but instead of taking rejection with integrity, they go about it in an underhanded way. They use an arsenal of tactics to emotionally strong-arm the other person into giving them what they want. They will use anything and everything they need to: your love for them, becoming pitiful, using intimidation, threats, and bribery, and even using mutual friends against you.

Over the course of this book, you will find out how to recognize you are in a relationship, whether it is romantic or platonic, with a narcissist, disentangle yourself from it, and deal with the consequences after doing so. You will also learn how to detect a narcissist in the future before you get invested in them.

If you recognize someone in your life to be a narcissist and still want to try to maintain a connection with them, let me give you this caution: narcissism is a chronic condition. That means it is lifelong and incurable. It can only be managed. This means they will always have the tendencies of this disorder.

They will never reach a point where they truly feel empathy for you. They can only imitate it.

They will need lifelong therapy where they will have to struggle to figure out what to say to you and how to respond to situations so that they come off as an empathetic person to you. They have to train themselves to take you into consideration and act in a way that is in your best interests. If they become lax with their therapy, medication, and coping mechanisms, they will fall back into old habits. Even if they follow this regimen rigorously, they will still struggle with narcissistic tendencies. This means it will be a constant battle for you.

Personality disorders are not something you can cure with love. Before you commit to a lifetime with anyone, you need to take a long hard look at the personality quirks and emotional baggage they come with and really think about whether or not this is something you can live with long term. These things will always be there no matter how much love and emotional energy you give to this person. Do not enter any sort of relationship with someone with the mindset that you are going to "fix" an aspect of them.

This is not something you have any power over. If a person is a narcissist, this manifested itself long before you came into the picture and if they want it to be treated, it will be up to them to make that happen. Only commit to a relationship with someone if you are happy with the person they are right now.

If you are already in a relationship with someone who is abusing you, emotionally or otherwise, heed this warning- it will not get better without intense cognitive behavioral therapy.

Unless and until they make the personal commitment to getting the treatment needed to manage their personality disorder, the abusive behavior will only get worse. You have probably heard the warnings about physically abusive partners, and how it will only get more dangerous over time to stay with them. The same lesson can be applied to emotional abuse. The longer you stay with a narcissist, the more oppressed you will be.

You will become increasingly isolated from your friends and family. Your hobbies and goals will go unattended. You will gradually lose bits of yourself.

We can appreciate the endearing movie storylines where the selfish friend or the inconsiderate spouse suddenly makes a miraculous turnaround and treats their loved ones better and they show gratitude to them for being patient enough to keep holding on all that time.

However, this is a fantasy. In reality, a narcissist will always be one. Your only hope of breaking the cycle of abuse in your own life is to sever your ties with them.

Chapter 6: Narcissistic Personality

By now, you have most likely heard of Narcissistic Personality Disorder. This disorder has been long misunderstood. They think of the tale of Narcissus, the man who fell in love with his own reflection. Because of this, for many years, people have thought the disorder was about a person looking in the mirror and talking about themselves all the time.

While they are often obsessed with their appearance and have notoriously self-centered dialogue, there is so much more to the disorder than that, and the impact it has on the people around them is so more profound.

The first thing you need to understand about Narcissistic Personality Disorder is that a person suffering from it is entirely focused on themselves. They are incapable of seeing things from another person's point of view.

If something is not of interest to them, it does not matter to them. If they do not see a potential use for them in another person, they do not matter to them.

They need to be the center of attention at all times. If something is not about them, they will manipulate the circumstances to where they force-fit it to be about them.

For example, if you are trying to talk to them about something that was done to you by someone else that upset, they will say something like "That reminds me of something that happened to me," and then go into detail about this event.

This turns it around into something where you are listening to them talk about their problems when it should have been a chance for you to talk about yours. Your feelings are neglected once again so theirs can be coddled.

This is why having a relationship with them is so dangerous. You will always be an afterthought for them. They will not care and probably will not even notice if they have done something that upsets you. Confronting them about it will only cause you more grief and frustration because if you can even get an acknowledgment out of them of what they did, they will turn it around to be your fault.

The impact someone with this personality disorder has on those who get emotionally invested in them is so high that it is known as narcissistic abuse. This is because the mistreatment goes so much deeper than talking only about themselves. When you think of other people you value them as a person, even if you are not emotionally invested in them.

You love your friends and family and are willing to make sacrifices for them, and if your relationship is healthy, they are willing to do the same things for you. Narcissists do not feel any of these things about anyone. They see other people as a means to an end.

Just like any other personality disorder, narcissism comes in different flavors. There are two primary forms a narcissist comes in: overt and covert.

The first one we will discuss is the overt, sometimes referred to as malignant, narcissist. This is the type that is the first to come to mind for most people at the mention of the word "narcissist". They are very blatant about their selfishness. Many of them recognize their personality disorder.

While some try to manage it, others embrace the symptoms and continue their destructive behaviors. They behave in a very similar fashion to the school bully tormenting younger, smaller children on the playground.

They have the mindset of a child. They expect to be given what they want when they want it, and if they do not get it, they will become angry. An overt narcissist is a control freak. They demand what they want from you in a loud and intimidating way.

It is arguable that a covert narcissist has the ability to cause even more damage than their overt counterparts. This is because they are entirely unaware of their narcissism. They portray themselves as the victim. In fact, they are often referred to as "victim narcissists." While overt narcissists openly make unreasonable demands, their covert counterparts use underhanded tactics to control others all the while portraying themselves as powerless.

You will be subjected to endless complaining about all of the people who have hurt them all throughout the course of their woe-ridden life. They do not wish to change their circumstances. Any suggestions you try to make for them to make better their situation will be met with "I wish I could do that, but..." and then they will go on to tell you another slew of problems that there are no solutions to.

There is something sinister about victimhood. We are not talking about actual victims. What we are talking about is a person that places themselves in bad situations and while they complain endlessly about them, they have no intention or even desire to better their lives. They enjoy blaming the world for their problems and lament about how much they could have been able to accomplish if it weren't for the things other people did to them.

Victim mentality means taking no ownership for your own circumstances. It also means the person spends a lot of time assigning blame in every direction but their own for their misfortunes. They present themselves as helpless and pitiful but are actually extremely angry people. They quietly seethe about what other people should have done for them and what no one has ever given themselves. A tell-tale sign you are talking to a covert narcissist is if they something along the lines of "I have never gotten a break in my life."

A relationship with a covert narcissist means you will never get an "I'm sorry too" after you have had an argument with them. You will apologize and they will withhold forgiveness until you have "truly earned it". In this way, the fight is never over. They have claimed permanent innocence.

You are the abuser and they are the victim. Even if they do admit to doing something unsavory, they will quickly explain that it was because of something you did. When they get angry at you, they are finally standing up for themselves after everything they have put up with from you.

The narcissistic supply for covert narcissists is the sympathy they get while they portray others as being evil. They will spend hours complaining to someone about you, and this is most likely the person they complain to you for hours at a time about. They often forget what they have said to which people, which is why you will most likely hear the same stories many times in a row.

At the core, a narcissist feels lowly about themselves, no matter what form they take on. The inflated self-importance comes from a place of trying to gain the self-worth that is missing within them. That is why they need supply in the first place. A person with self-esteem that comes from an internal place does not need anyone else to be lower than them to feel self-confidence.

In fact, they aim to lift the spirits of the people around them. That is why a narcissist is a pitiful person despite all of their viciousness, and they should be viewed that way. They are not powerful no matter how loud they shout or how scathing their words are.

You cannot have a healthy relationship where your emotional needs are being met with a narcissist. They do not have the capacity to genuinely care about the wants and needs of anyone but their own selves. This means they cannot feel empathy for other people.

They cannot see another person's perspective and they are not motivated to try to relate to others. To commit to an interpersonal relationship with them means you are going to be on an endless and unreciprocated journey of building them up.

The exact set of circumstances that create narcissistic personality disorder is unknown. Many psychologists believe it comes from a mixture of genetic predisposition and environmental factors. Abuse and neglect often play a role in the development of a personality disorder.

Overt narcissists were often raised by one and while they were excessively praised and indulged, their emotional needs were not met. They were taught that love is conditional. Their parents would appreciate them whenever they did well, but this love and affection would vanish if they failed at something, and it would be made known to them that they let the family down.

This turned them into what is sometimes referred to as an "approval junkie". They need constant validation from others because they do not have their own self-esteem to rely on.

Covert narcissists often come from an abusive background where their needs were not met and they were not praised. They learned that the only way they could get something they wanted or needed was through manipulation. They thrust themselves into situations where they are the victim as an adult.

You will most likely have heard many tales of woe from a covert narcissist within a very short time of knowing them. You will listen to the stories of their childhood and adulthood, and there was never a good day in either of those timelines according to them.

There will be an entire cluster of names of people you are not supposed to talk to because they did this person wrong. In fact, they will require it of you to hate these people despite never having spoken to them before.

Be very wary of people who point someone out before you meet them and say something along the lines of "Watch out for them, they have mental problems". This is likely a person they are running a smear campaign against. We will delve deeper into what a smear campaign is later in the book.

A narcissist is a pathological liar by nature. You will not get the truth out of them. They live by the rule that the truth is what they say it is. A pathological liar is defined as someone who lies compulsively. This means not only do they have a habit of lying, but it is an addiction. They get a thrill out of it when they lie. Everyone has told a lie before. Maybe someone asked you if you liked their shirt and you said yes so you wouldn't hurt their feelings. Perhaps you hid a bad grade from your parents. For many teenagers, there is one time or another where they lie to their parents. If you are alive in this world, there are things you had said before that were untrue. When you did this, you probably felt guilty.

You value the person you lied to and you know what you did was wrong. This is because you have empathy. This is something a narcissist lacks.

In fact, they think lowly of the people they are lying to. They look down on them for not having the intelligence to see through their deceit, even though they are going to every length possible to avoid the other person knowing the truth.

You need to be warned about entering a relationship with a narcissist. They are invariably unfaithful to their partners. This is because they do not see romantic relationships in the same way others do. It is not a commitment that is about love and trust for them. As dramatic as their relationships tend to be, they have a very shallow view of them. They do not have it in them to go through a real relationship.

They want the first few months where everything is easy and it is all fun and games. When it comes time to create a deeper commitment, they do not want this. They do not want to give themselves to someone else.

When the narcissist is caught in the act of infidelity, they will not take ownership for their actions. You will never get an apology or remorse from them. Instead, they will tell their partners it was their fault that they cheated. One of the most common reasons they will give is that their partner was not having sex with them, not taking into consideration at all the idea that their poor treatment of the other person is what is making them not want to have sex with them.

They might also say they were feeling ignored. Whatever the wording of the excuse was, their needs were not being met and it is their partner's fault that they went astray.

There is a correlation between narcissism and sex addiction. This is not to say all narcissists have it, or that everyone with sex addiction is a narcissist. However, a narcissist is prone to sex addiction. They will often have a fixation on pornography. It is not uncommon that they have a large number of sexual partners even if they are in a relationship.

Most people see sex as a meaningful thing that you do not share with someone unless there is some form of attachment to them. For a narcissist, sex is a conquest and it is also something they use to manipulate people.

Both men and women can be manipulated by sex. They often mistake the pleasure of the act for attachment and emotional vulnerability. There are often words spoken during sex that are very tender, grand declarations of love. For a healthy relationship, the act of sex should be a means of expressing love and it does bring people closer. For a narcissist, they use it to obtain forgiveness they have not earned. They use it to make a person feel like they are close.

If you have ever been in a relationship where your partner was unfaithful to you, it was not your fault. When a person is cheated on, they are the victim.

They are blameless. If someone chooses to look outside of their own relationship for romance and sex, that is their decision. If they had some sort of complaint about you, they should have gone to you about it. Their infidelity had nothing to do with you and everything to do with them. It says something about their character, not yours. It means they cannot keep a commitment they have made. They were planning to be unfaithful from the very start. While they will string you along, a narcissist is figuring out how and when they are going to discard you from the time you first seemingly start getting closer.

The tendency to be a pathological liar contributes to a narcissist's ability to cheat on their partner. For a person without a narcissistic personality disorder, if they found themselves in a situation where they have a connection with a person other than their partner that is crossing a boundary, they would feel a deep sense of guilt and want to fix this situation.

They would eventually make the decision to either come clean to their partner about the infidelity, and try to work things out from there, or they would break up with their partner if they realized they had fallen in love with someone else and wanted a relationship with them.

For a narcissist, they do not mind living a double life. In fact, there is a sort of satisfaction they get out of lying to their partner and maybe even the people they see outside of their relationship.

Another thing to understand about lying is that it is not always about what the person says. Sometimes it is about what they do not say. You have probably heard of the term "lying by omission." This means the story a person is telling is a lie because of the fact that they are telling a small portion of the truth. The detail they left out would tell a completely different story from the one they are trying to make everyone believe.

An example of lying by omission is a child telling their father that their mother yelled at them for no reason. When the father asks his wife what happened he finds out she had asked the child to clean his room a week ago and it had still not been done.

A narcissist often lies by omission when they are telling other people stories about the things their victims did.

They will tell everyone about irrational things the other person did while they conveniently forget to talk about their part in the exchange. They might tell a group of friends "They've been messaging me all day. They're crazy!" The detail of the story they do not share is that the person lent them a large amount of money and they have failed to pay their debt.

Before we start to discuss narcissism in-depth, there is a disclaimer that needs to be made. Acting in self-interest is not narcissism. In fact, there is an argument that there is a "healthy level of narcissism." This means you care about self-preservation and that you will not let yourself be depleted by other people.

Following this theory, if there are no narcissistic traits present within you, it means you are in victim mode, which means there is no part of you that is interested in helping yourself and will let others mistreat and take advantage of you. Some argue that victim mode is unhealthier than any level of narcissism. However, a victim mentality is a form of narcissism in its own right.

This is because when you are in this mode, you are thinking entirely of yourself. You've probably met people who wallow in a "poor me" mindset. These people have deep selfishness because they can only think about their pain and see the suffering of others as being nothing compared to theirs.

In fact, covert narcissism is a person who is in permanent victim mode. They say "why does this always happen to me" and "why will no one ever give me the breaks that everyone else gets". They never think about what they can do to better their lives. Their mind plays a constant loop of "I wish I could, but I can't, and this is why". You cannot lift them up enough. In fact, they do not want to be lifted up. They only want to drag you down.

Conclusion

Human behavior is a complex subject that is deep as it is wide. Understanding human behavior needs you to learn various skills, and then when you decide to influence the behavior, you ought to look at the multiple aspects that make it possible for you to have an impact on someone.

Human behavior refers to the character of a person. You adopt the behavior as you grow – from your parents, school, peers, and other people in the community. This is why you have heard so often it is mentioned that someone is of "good" or "bad" behavior. The way you behave right away tells someone a little about your upbringing.

The good thing is that you can change your behavior; however, it takes more than just stopping something for a few hours or days – it takes all your willpower and effort to change your behavior.

Let us look at the factors that can make someone change their behavior:

Willpower

Before someone can decide to change their behavior, they should genuinely want to change it. They need to have the willpower to make decisions and stick to them. When someone has the desire to change, they discipline themselves to follow the plans through.

Changing behavior starts with a plan, and when you have the desire to change the behavior, you need the strength to stick to this plan even when you feel like giving up.
It also works the other way round, in order for you to persuade someone to change their behavior; they need to be willing to do so; otherwise, you will be wasting your time.

Knowledge and Skills

When you come up with plans to do something, you need to have the knowledge and skills to succeed. For instance, when you decide to lose weight, yet you don't have the expertise to do so, you might end up failing.

With the right skills and knowledge to achieve a decision, you will be able to direct your willpower more effectively.

To apply this aspect, you need to try and educate the people that you are trying to persuade so that they have the right knowledge to handle the issue at hand.

They need to commit to a plan that will give them the right results. After they put the plan in motion, the next step is to make sure they can monitor their progress the right way.

Social Motivation

This is another prime factor that influences the way we act. Most of us have evolved to fit in a crowd because this crowd has helped us to stay safe. Many people around you will help you to stay motivated and accountable, while others will seek to make you stray from your goals.

When persuading people, you need to help them realize that the people around them can be their allies or accomplices when they pursue their goals. Make sure you teach them how to communicate with the people around them well.

Social Ability

This is the capacity to accomplish something that you have never done through finding someone that has already done it before successfully. This means looking for a mentor, a support group, or a coach to guide you.

This is why, as a persuasion expert, you are there to help someone find his footing so as to change behavior.

CPSIA information can be obtained
at www.ICGtesting.com
Printed in the USA
BVHW041346220421
605633BV00005B/1197